T0078023

Love *of* Light

A GUIDE TO PEACE AND ONENESS

LISA COLLINS, ED.D

ARCHWAY
PUBLISHING

Copyright © 2022 Lisa Collins, Ed.D.

All rights reserved. No part of this book may be used or reproduced by
any means, graphic, electronic, or mechanical, including photocopying,
recording, taping or by any information storage retrieval system
without the written permission of the author except in the case of
brief quotations embodied in critical articles and reviews.

This book is a work of non-fiction. Unless otherwise noted, the author
and the publisher make no explicit guarantees as to the accuracy of
the information contained in this book and in some cases, names of
people and places have been altered to protect their privacy.

Archway Publishing books may be ordered through booksellers or by contacting:

Archway Publishing
1663 Liberty Drive
Bloomington, IN 47403
www.archwaypublishing.com
844-669-3957

Because of the dynamic nature of the Internet, any web addresses or
links contained in this book may have changed since publication and
may no longer be valid. The views expressed in this work are solely those
of the author and do not necessarily reflect the views of the publisher,
and the publisher hereby disclaims any responsibility for them.

Any people depicted in stock imagery provided by Getty Images are
models, and such images are being used for illustrative purposes only.
Certain stock imagery © Getty Images.

Scripture quotations are from the New Revised Standard Version Bible, copyright
© 1989 the Division of Christian Education of the National Council of the
Churches of Christ in the United States of America.
Used by permission. All rights reserved.

ISBN: 978-1-6657-2146-2 (sc)
ISBN: 978-1-6657-2147-9 (e)

Library of Congress Control Number: 2022906112

Print information available on the last page.

Archway Publishing rev. date: 04/25/2022

Contents

Introduction

In this twenty-first century it is difficult to connect spiritually. With technology and the high speed of the world today, people find themselves lost. The lack of community in a spiritual form is lacking and people are doing whatever they can to connect to something. Desperate for spiritual connection, they seek out activities such as extreme sports, where people put their lives on the line in the name of sport, and antics like reality TV shows in which people put their lives at stake to survive in the wilderness or stage a living arrangement or a romantic relationship.

It is noticeable that the church has repelled society, as most people do not attend church or seek spiritual assistance there. The uptick in spirituality as a movement and yoga as a semi-spiritual practice in America demonstrates that the yearning for something not of this world is present in society. At the same time, it is apparent that extremism of religiosity has captured people in such a way that it is harmful and fear-based, which is not of God. How did we get in such a space where we are repelled by one another and smite each other for such worldly reasons as sexuality, political thoughts, or skin color? The world is in need of peace and love, and that comes in the form of God. What is God? God is love. This is simple enough, and although it is written in the Bible, it does not transfer to practice.

Why is it so difficult to love one another? It seems easy enough, but instead we seem to listen to the deep-seated voice that we are not one—we are separate and therefore need to fend for ourselves. Through this dynamic, everyone is "othered." Think about your day-to-day life: when a person cuts you off in their car on the freeway or street, do you slow down and let them go or curse them for their actions? Who has not acted this way? How hard is it for all of us just to surrender the space and be happy and grateful we are not hurt? This world drives us to go inward toward individuality and self when God's words and wisdom ask us to be one with God and our brothers and sisters.

The change needed will be a drastic one. One in which people are intentionally moving from the fortress of self, bunkers, and protection to love and inclusivity, starting with prayer for others. The first step is to pray for others—all others—and not in the way which is known today. The prayer is silent, without words, connecting to God and allowing God to speak to you. In this silent time, pray for others, and feel that connection and warmth for your own healing. Send good thoughts for other people; do not judge them, try to control the solution for them, or pity them. Simply send good thoughts their way.

Look at others as if they are whole. What a concept! What would happen if we examined all as if they were whole? The warmth of the love we had for them would be present because they are nothing more. There's no need to understand everything that happens; that is not our place. Our place is to love, become one with God, and seek to not let our mind and ego control us.

A Course In Miracles (1977) was given to our world long ago. It describes and teaches solid ways of being that lead to enlightenment. The many cults of our centuries show us that we are seeking that special place where we are enlightened, and we are looking for a person to lead us. We are the person. Enlightenment begins with us individually. The course tells us that we must deal with our minds. Think about the psychology of today people are seeking, self-care, self-esteem, and self-regulation, which together translates into some form of peace. Peace is found through oneness with God, and all the psychology books in the world will not bring the peace the world is seeking. The more we drill into ourselves, the more harm is committed to ourselves and others. It has to be this way: we cannot take care of ourselves fully by putting others aside. A huge right or left turn will need to occur for most people to feel, hear, and answer God's call of oneness. What should we do?

The first thing to do is to pray. As mentioned earlier, prayer has developed into ways in which one sits and reads or repeats phrases. The act of contemplative prayer has gone by the wayside. Our brother, Richard Rohr, has made a lifetime practice of assisting people to connection and oneness with God. His work is pleasing and necessary. He has touched many people, and some have been enlightened. Other brothers Desmond Tutu and the Dalai Lama also have forged forward as examples displaying love and oneness with God. Both of these spiritual leaders participate in prayer as mentioned earlier every day for many hours. That upper room with God is a precious one and we are fooled if we think we are surviving spiritually without this great comfort.

The second thing we must do is control the darkness of our minds. Judgment, our terrible friend, has to be put to rest. This is the basic and first projection we must be rid of in our life on earth. The Bible is very clear on judgment: "Judge not" (Matthew 7:1). Yet our world is based on and engulfed in judgment and judgmental practices as media, entertainment, and a way of being. It is normal to assess people's character, clothes, lives, and family. It is so normed for us in this world that we have entire institutions for judging others: newspapers, magazines, television shows, etc. School attendance, workplace relations, and even employment in the church are based on judgment, criteria, and a long list of things that basically fall into people perceptions.

We have made a life of Judgment. It is time to pull back and lead with love. What would it be like if you, not your neighbor, lead with love instead of judgment? It is hard and takes practice. It is a continuum, not a destination, but prayer can bring a peace that I think people are looking for through Etsy, eBay, Pinterest, Facebook, Instagram, entertainment centers, twice-a-year church, and fitness crazes, to name a few.

We have spent so much time on the body, which will perish at some point, and no time on the spirit, which will last us forever. The body focus is so obtuse that a clear change of direction is needed in our society. It is understandable that fear and man-made destruction have harmed and terrorized people within the church systems, and people's thoughts, deeds, and actions have made the church not welcoming or attractive for those seeking spiritual refuge.

Let us pause here and heal from what has been man-made issues using God as a shield. God is not the problem here, and the organized church has a very human-centered and worldly way of thinking and doing. Do not get me wrong; church institutions do a lot of good works, and the part of the church grounded in this world more that the spiritual has caused much harm and sadness. That being said, the realignment of spiritual practices first and foremost is a necessary action the churches in the world must take in order to meet their goal of spiritual oneness with God for their own sake and for humankind.

A Course in Miracles is a basic text, and it offers healing and lessons with instructions how to learn. Yet many people out there have not been reached or touched by the messaging clearly written in its pages. Therefore, here we will reframe some of the concepts to reach society in a different way. Again, our stress will be a focus on prayer first as a foundation for spiritual connection and oneness with God. Each person is so loved and carries the possibility and warmth of love with them, yet they have not reached out to pull the love of God onto their souls.

The first part of this book will explain prayer and teach you how to pray. The second part of this book will give practical solutions for dealing with judgment in today's society. Judgment has reached a point of pure destruction and continues to be projected everywhere, from the pulpits to children's lunchrooms. The third part of this book will address the need for healing communities and how to begin to convene in a way that is pleasing to God and provides healing justice to this hurting world.

I write these things as a prophet of the word of God, not an authority or proclaimed person who knows all. I have my own story of redemption that has nothing to do with the words of this work. I have been called from above to write this book in the name of God to proclaim healing in this world and offer some tools for those who are interested in coming nearer to our Creator. I have no interest in being an authority but am a faithful servant who serves as called, and I am grateful for the opportunity.

Chapter 1

There are many scholars and proclaimed experts on the Word of God. At this point in time, the books, study guides, and commentaries are plentiful. What is missing in our world today are practical actions and practices that bring about healing and end suffering.

There seems to be an obsession with the suffering of others in this world, so much so that countless charities are looking to help ease suffering in the world. This is good, but where is the soul work for those suffering and those assisting? The focus on worldly life is overabundant at this time. Although charities provide healing work or assistance for the less fortunate, they are missing a major tenet of what Jesus has taught us. (The reference to Jesus does not discount any other references to a higher being such as Allah, Jehovah, or Yahweh.) Jesus taught us to know God, and the continued work in this world in the name of God is not propagating the knowledge of God for ourselves or the people we are helping. Are we sitting down with those we are helping to pray silently to God, or are we assisting them and moving on to the next people in the name of God? Should people be without food and water? No. But where are we connecting with humankind's spirit to touch our Lord above? The answer is simple and obvious. We are not doing so; that is the purpose of this writing.

God is pleased with the altruistic actions of feeding the hungry, clothing the children, and caring for the sick; this is all within the words that have been left here for us to read and study. Yet the spirit has been neglected in these centuries since the Bible, which has humankind's hands all over it, since it was written. It is good to use the Bible as a resource, but where is the connection to God and spirit? We have truly let the words and humankind's interpretation rule our understanding of the Bible and our actions based on it. People are ostracized, hated, and "othered" because of words in the Bible. This displeases God and has to come to an end.

It is not for us to understand everyone's existence, whether they be transgender, questioning, or fluid. What is important is that all people, no matter who they are, will have to connect spiritually through prayer if they are seeking oneness with God. Prayer has been lost in today's world. Big words are thrown about among us, and little time is spent in the upper room of our consciousness with a higher power. For those who read this book and want to be held in the arms of your Creator, please read on. It will assist you and hopefully those who come in contact with you along your journey.

Are verbal prayers useless? No. That is not what is being written here. Some of the most beautiful poems for God have been written throughout time. Those poems of love come from silent communion with our Lord. But in our world, those words, poems, and sayings have replaced what is supposed to be time spent with God. Humankind's words have morphed into workshops on prosperity, marriage, and child-rearing instead of the oneness that we all need to connect to a higher being and bring ourselves out of suffering.

What steps are needed to begin? Simply, one needs to make time for God every day. This is quite a suggestion in the midst of our daily hurried schedules, but it is necessary to make a connection. We have forgotten who we are. No matter what you believe—whether you are an atheist or an agnostic, a Jew or a Christian—you have to stop and spend time with God. It is quite simple. It is the first part of making a connection. We make many excuses for not having time or space, but we must make the time and spend it quietly without any words. We have experienced bread crumbs along the way. The book *Fervent* speaks of praying fervently about the issues in a marriage. The word *fervent* means "having or displaying a passionate intensity." This passion is needed when we take time out every day for prayer. One does not need words, a scripture, or a special reading. Prayer is accessible to all people everywhere.

Prayer Practice

Make sure you are able to have some time to yourself. If you are partnered or married, you can eventually connect with your spouse or partner, but you should always have your own personal time of prayer. Please do not shy away from asking children to take quiet time (not the punishing time-out or reflection worksheets used in schools). Children are naturally close to God and spirit. The way they move in the world is something to admire, not control. Children have a peace beyond understanding most of the time. We have a lot to learn from them. Encourage them from the youngest of ages to sit with you quietly until they are able to do this on their own as part of their prayer time. How often do we ask children to pause and take a moment? We ourselves are not doing so. Let's begin to practice and model prayer for those in our lives.

There are some things that will assist your connection with a higher power: fragrances, darkness, quiet, soft low-frequency music, and an undisturbed setting. This is not an exhaustive list but a starting point. There is a wide range of possibilities, and it is important to get ideas from this text. However, it is not a how-to guide. Your spirit will guide you toward what is best for your personal practice. If you are using fragrances, it important to research what you choose and what properties it possesses.

Once you have carved out quiet time in your busy life, begin with ten minutes of sitting. This requires a blank mind, which means you are not going over the grocery list, what the neighbor or guy at work said, or how you are feeling. Yes, it requires practice, and it does take time. That is why the world has shifted to the use of set prayers, even though the Lord's Prayer, which is a guide, has become an institution for Christian societies. Prayer connection requires a commitment to your spirit—remember that part.

At this point in the book, work on mastering ten minutes of sitting in silence before reading on. Many will read on to see what is next; this is a result of the hectic pace of our world. Try not to. Trust in your higher self, and get ten minutes of quiet under your belt every day. This commitment is to your higher self and your spiritual connection to God. Worldly punishment, shaming, and humiliation are not part of this love practice. Warmth and gentleness are part of this practice. Do not give up your connection to your higher self; it is worth it. When you feel a warmth like being cuddled in a blanket by a warm fire, or whatever warmth and love feel like for you, that is the connection. Once you reach it, you will want it more and more because it's healing and feeds the higher spirit, allowing you to deal with the worldly troubles that weave in and out of your time here.

Incorporating Inspiration

Once you have established a prayer life, quiet time every day where a connection is felt with a higher power, inspiration can be added to your practice. Inspiration can include word poems, known prayers, scripture, the Koran, the Torah, or great writings. It is very important to have the quiet time established before adding inspirational text. The text should be something that speaks to you. If it sparks a feeling inside when you read it, that is a touchstone. It should not be something you pick because you learned it growing up and you feel attached to it by obligation. Pick something that sings to your soul. Do not be afraid to look outside your chosen organized religion or faith. There are some beautiful indigenous writings, phrases, and sayings, as well as a plethora of inspiration throughout the world.

Prayers

Greatest Light among the World, Wind of Love and Comfort,
Hear my prayer and calling to be closer
to you in every way, every day.
Make me like the eagle that flies, and carry me
in the comfort of your arms and love
As I wander in the way you would have me.
In your eyes and in your walk, ground me like
the great trees, flowers, and earth.
Let me bring peace and kindness to all in
graciousness, just as you do for me.
Allow me to touch the oneness of the earth,
and let my spirt fly like the wind.

Dearest and most precious Light,
I thank you for my rising and slumber.
O precious Mother,
Hold me in your grasp as I wallow on this earth.
Let me see your ever-bright light of love, hope, and comfort
In everyone I see and those whose lives I touch.
Allow me to be one with you.

The love of one another is one that I seek.
O Light of light, Love of love,
Show me the way of oneness with those who
love me and those who smite me.
Be it my love of you in me that revels in the heights of
bliss as I become one in love and light in your name.

Mother God, in the essence of your will,
Continue to provide love and light in my heart.

Help me set aside my needs as I continue to push
for more love among those who hate me.
I love them with more passion every day, as it is through my love
of you in me that I transcend to oneness within this world.

Father God, in your name I call on the light of all light
And the intense love of the pure light to bless each and
every one in the spirit world and the earth plane.
Let the radiant flow of abundance in a loving
spirit overturn the wrath of evil.
It is love at the deepest level that holds us all, and only
love will save us all from the torment of ourselves.
Light of light, love of love, enter me right now.

Rise up and sing the song of gratefulness
As you know where your strength comes from.
The goodness of each of us is within;
Rise up and sing the song of gratefulness.
Praise the goodness of your heart;
Love the plentifulness of your existence,
For this love is your nourishment and salvation.

Turn toward love,
Turn toward care,
Turn toward the depth of love God has for you.
See the love in your life;
See the love in your existence. Turn toward the love.

It is not what you think, this walk of life.
Take time to see what you cannot see;
Take time to love what you have not loved.
Take time to breathe in the love and light of it all.

Below are some I have found as I have researched:

A Native Prayer you may want to use while smudging:
Creator, Great Mystery Source of all knowing and comfort, Cleanse this space of all negativity. Open our pathways to peace and understanding. Love and light fills each of us and our sacred space. Our work here shall be beautiful and meaningful. Banish all energies that would mean us harm. Our eternal gratitude.
– *The Medicine Wheel Garden,* E. Barrie Kavasch

The Great Spirit Prayer
Oh, Great Spirit, whose voice I hear in the wind, whose breath gives life to all the world.

Hear me; I need your strength and wisdom.

Let me walk in beauty, and make my eyes ever behold the red and purple sunset.

Make my hands respect the things you have made and my ears sharp to hear your voice.

Make me wise so that I may understand the things you have taught my people.

Help me to remain calm and strong in the face of all that comes towards me.

Let me learn the lessons you have hidden in every leaf and rock.

Help me seek pure thoughts and act with the intention of helping others.

— translated by Chief Yellow Lark

"Regret is an appalling waste of energy; you can't build on it; it's only good for wallowing in." — Katherine Mansfield; excerpt from Al-Anon Family Groups, "Courage to Change"

"We must alter our lives in order to alter our hearts, for it is impossible to live one way and pray another." —William Law; excerpt from Al-Anon Family Groups, "Courage to Change"

"God's will is duty at the present moment." — Classical Devotion – Foster & Smith

The Shehecheyanu – Recite this blessing the first time you do something each Jewish calendar year (e.g., the first night of Hanukkah when you light the menorah), and to mark joyous occasions. "Blessed are You, Lord our God, King of the Universe, who has granted us life, sustained us and enabled us to reach this occasion." *https:// reformjudaism.org/practice/prayers-blessings/shehecheyanu*

Oh God, my prayer-of-now, let me not abandon to despair.
Oh Mother, give me strength to do what e'er I can.
Grant that those I touch each day may feel my core of hope,
The stubborn refusal to let destruction win.
Oh God, give me courage to endure this time of trial.
Oh Mother, guide my hands and heart to peace.
—"In a Violent Age" – Rev. Maureen Killoran – 2008

Lord, take me where You want me to go;
Let me meet who You want me to meet;
Tell me what You want me to say; and
Keep me out of Your way.
— Father Mychal Judge, FDNY – died 9/11/01

Daily Prayer of the Soul- nur nurbha
Lord, make pure my intentions for this prayer …
Let us strive with our tongue and our deeds to earn your mercy.
Sway our hearts towards U so that our limbs may follow.
Prevent us from distractions that will harm our mind, body and soul.
Guide us to your straight path.
Let this transient life be an opportunity to grow spiritually,
And bring us out of ignorance into Light (Nur).
Ameen

Adapted bedtime prayer – Doris Howe
Keep far from me at night
All things that me affright
And wake me safe with sunshine bright
within my heart;
If not within my sight.

Psalm of David - Psalm 61:1–4
Hear my cry, O God;
listen to my prayer.
From the ends of the earth I call to you,
I call as my heart grows faint;
lead me to the rock that is higher than I.
For you have been my refuge,
a strong tower against the foe
I long to dwell in your tent forever
and take refuge in the shelter of your wings.

Romans 12:12
Be joyful in hope, patient in affliction, faithful in prayer.

Romans 15:13
May the God of hope fill you with all joy and peace as you trust in him, so that you may overflow with hope by the power of the Holy Spirit.

Psalm 62:5-6
Let all that I am wait quietly before God,
for my hope is in him.
He alone is my rock and my salvation,
my fortress where I will not be shaken.

"God, grant me the grace to pause between the impulse and the action...."

Isaiah 54:10
"For the mountains may be removed and the hills may shake,
But My loving kindness will not be removed from you,
And My covenant of peace will not be shaken,"
Says the Lord who has compassion on you.

Philippians 4:6-7
Be anxious for nothing, but in everything by prayer and supplication with thanksgiving let your requests be made known to God. And the peace of God, which surpasses all comprehension, will guard your hearts and your minds in Christ Jesus.

"When you feel at the mercy of your circumstances, ask for My Peace before you ask for anything else."

Psalm 119:11
I have hidden your word in my heart that I might not sin against you.

Philippians 4:4, 12

Rejoice in the Lord always. I will say it again: Rejoice! ... I know what it is to be in need, and I know what it is to have plenty. I have learned the secret of being content in any and every situation, whether well fed or hungry, whether living in plenty or in want. — Excerpt From Sarah Young, *Jesus Calling* (Thomas Nelson, 2015)

Ephesians 3:16–19"

I pray that out of his glorious riches he may strengthen you with power through his Spirit in your inner being, so that Christ may dwell in your hearts through faith. And I pray that you, being rooted and established in love, may have power, together with all the saints, to grasp how wide and long and high and deep is the love of Christ, and to know this love that surpasses knowledge—that you may be filled to the measure of all the fullness of God.

Book of Common Prayer 58. For Guidance, Rite One

O God, by whom the meek are guided in judgment, and light riseth up in darkness for the godly: Grant us, in all our doubts and uncertainties, the grace to ask what thou wouldest have us to do, that the Spirit of wisdom may save us from all false choices, and that in thy light we may see light, and in thy straight path may not stumble; through Jesus Christ our Lord. Amen.

1 Thessalonians 5:16–18

Rejoice always; pray without ceasing; in everything give thanks; for this is God's will for you in Christ Jesus.

Joshua 1:5

No one will be able to stand against you all the days of your life. As I was with Moses, so I will be with you; I will never leave you nor forsake you.

Psalm 143:8
Let me hear of your loving-kindness in the morning
for I put my trust in you; *
show me the road that I must walk,
for I lift up my soul to you.

Psalm 40:2
He drew me up out of a horrible pit [a pit of tumult and of destruction],
out of the miry clay (froth and slime), and set my feet upon a rock,
steadying my steps *and* establishing my goings. —AMPC

Reflect on the psalms of David: They show that genuine faith is not
canceled out by fear. — Sarah Young, *Jesus Calling Morning and
Evening Devotional* (Thomas Nelson, 2015)

Romans 8:15–16
For you did not receive a spirit that makes you a slave again to fear,
but you received the Spirit of sonship. And by him we cry, "Abba,
Father." The Spirit himself testifies with our spirit that we are God's
children.

What you resist persist. — Carl Jung

Desmond Tutu, Book of African Prayers

Today Is God
In the beginning was God,
Today is God,
Tomorrow will be God.
Who can make an image of God?
He has no body.
He is the word which comes out of your mouth.
That word! It is no more,

It is past, and still it lives!
So is God. — Pygmy

I Have No Words to Thank You, O My Father, Great Elder
I have no words to thank you,
But with your deep wisdom
I am sure that you can see
How I value your glorious gifts.
O my Father, when I look upon your greatness,
I am confounded with awe.
O Great Elder,
Ruler of all things earthly and heavenly,
I am your warrior,
Ready to act in accordance with your will. — Kikuyu, Kenya

Chords of Praise
I shall sing a song of praise to God:
Strike the chords upon the drum.
God who gives us all good things—
Strike the chords upon the drum—
Wives, and wealth, and wisdom.
Strike the chords upon the drum. — Baluba, Zaire

The Source of Being Is Above
The source of being is above,
which gives life to all people;
For people are satisfied, and do not die of famine,
For the Lord gives them life,
that they may live prosperously
on the earth and not die of famine. — Zulu, South Africa

Thank You Very Much!
Thank you very, very much;

my God, thank you.
Give me food today,
food for my sustenance every day.
Thank you very, very much. — Samburu, Kenya

Make Us Instruments of Your Faith
For your blessing we thank you, God: faith in you,
Increase it, we beg, so that we no longer doubt.
Drive out all our miserliness, so that we do not
refuse you anything.
Increase our faith, for the sake of those without faith.
Make us instruments of your faith, for those with
only a little.
Fill our bodies with faith, our bodies that work for
you all our days.
Help us to avoid the enemies of our faith, or to
overcome them. You are with us in confrontations; this we believe.
In your hands we place ourselves, and are secure.
Make haste to enter our hearts; make haste
in me. May I go through the day calling on you, you, O Lord, who
know no other Lord. — Galla, Ethiopia

God Free You
May God free you; may God guard you night and day.
May God set you in your right place, and may you
spread out like the grass of a prairie. Spread out like palm leaves;
continue your walk,
and may life be with you.
May God place you where God's stars are placed
at dawn and at night.
Spread out like water of a lake.
Be numerous like the feet of a millipede. — Samburu, Kenya

Prayer: Creed

We grow from the Earth
And we share Her fruits.
We fly with bright wings
And we reach the stars.
We are Immortal with all that is.
Evoe Isis!

In this passage, the ancient Egyptians worship Isis in this creed. They proclaim that they are the followers and disciples of Isis as they recite this prayer, while offering worship to her.

Prayer: Thanksgiving

Holy Isis, Holy Osiris;
We give you thanks
that your Love, Beauty and Truth
Are manifest with Power and Peace
throughout all spheres,
within all beings,
and we accept your Blessing now,
in Mind and Heart.

This prayer is one of thanksgiving and perhaps of blessing. Again we see that Osiris and Isis were important to the ancient Egyptians during spiritual prayer and ritual. (E. Sanchez)

https://sites.google.com/a/smpanthers.org/fulay-6th-period-scripture/home/ancient-egyptian-prayers-and-ritual-worship

pg. xx
The beauty of the trees,
The softness of the air,

The fragrance of the grass speaks to me.
The summit of the mountains,
The thunder of the sky,
The rhythm of the sea,
Speaks to me, and my heart soaks ….

Pg. 1 The mountains, I become part of it the herbs the fir tree, I become part of it. The morning mists, the clouds, the gathering waters, I become part of it.

The mountains, I become part of it …
The herbs, the fir tree ….

Follow the Light.

https://en.wikisource.org/wiki/A Treasury of South African Poetry and Verse/Religious and Metaphysical poems

A dewdrop in shade of slenderest blade;
A foam-flake on verge of mountainous surge;

Delusive lake where deserts bake,
Or passing shade by an eagle made;

One golden ray on a wintry day;
A cloud's brief bliss 'neath the sunset-kiss.

Life's toil and strain but this to gain!
When lasting treasure no thought can measure

He may surely find, who with steadfast mind
Keeps trimmed and bright the Inward Light.

That Light may lead where feet shall bleed,
And voices drear assail the ear,

When horrid sights shall throng the nights,
And days be rife with fears and strife.

The treasure by thee will be found, maybe,
Amid the rattle and smoke of battle.
Or far it may lie 'neath a flickering sky
'Mid wastes ablaze in the scorching rays.

Perchance it peers where Winter rears
In the Arctic zone his eternal throne;

Or far, it may be, 'neath the purple sea
On a weltering steep of the sunless deep.

But how or where be not thy care:
That priceless treasure no thought can measure,

He shall surely find who with steadfast mind
Keeps trimmed and bright the Inward Light.

Through toil, through pain, in loss, in gain,
By day, by night, follow the Light. — Thich Nhat Hanh

May I be peaceful, light & happy in body & in mind.

May I be free & safe from accidents.

May I be free from anger, unwholesome states of mind & worries.

May I know how to look at myself with the eyes of understanding
& love.

May I be able to recognize & touch the seeds of joy & happiness in myself.

May I learn how to nourish myself with joy each day.

May I be able to live fresh, solid & free.

May I not be caught in the state of indifference or be caught in the extremes

of attachment or aversion.

May you be peaceful, light & happy in body & in mind.

May you be free and safe from accidents.

May you be free from anger, unwholesome states of mind & worries.

May you know how to look at yourself with the eyes of understanding & love.

May you be able to recognize and touch the seeds of joy & happiness in yourself.

May you learn how to nourish yourself with joy each day.

May you be able to live fresh, solid & free.

May you not be caught in the state of indifference or be caught in the extremes

of attachment or aversion.

May all beings be peaceful, light & happy in body & in mind.

May all beings be free & safe from accidents.

May all beings be free from anger, unwholesome states of mind & worries.

May all beings know how to look at themselves with the eyes of understanding & love.

May all beings be able to recognize & touch the seeds of joy and happiness in themselves.

May all beings learn how to nourish themselves with joy each day.

May all beings be able to live fresh, solid & free.

May all beings not be caught in the state of indifference or be caught in the extremes

of attachment or aversion. — Thich Nhat Hanh

Share this:

https://prayersmantrasspirituallyrics.wordpress.com/2011/02/20/thich-nhat-hanh/

Prayer to be chanted on waking up

Karāgre vasate lakṣmeeh,
Karamūle saraswatee;
Karamadhye tu govindah,
Prabhāte karadarśanam.

"On the tips of the fingers is Goddess Lakshmi, on the base of the fingers is Goddess Saraswati, in the middle of the fingers is Lord Govinda."

I am attracting and sending loving healing energy with every step I take today.   Sohini Sinha

Evelyn Lim: "I am fearless." If you said this out loud, it would be very effective to raise your voice and emphasize the word *fearless*. If you raise your hand in a strong gesture, it further anchors the strength and courage that you feel in your body. The visual image that may go along with "I am fearless" could be seeing yourself confronting a strong adversary and looking right into his or her eyes and feeling in your heart that you are too strong to cower and that you are planted firmly to the Earth.

Chapter 2

Prayer in ancient times served a different purpose than the need of prayer today. Today, society has completely lost touch with the spirit, so a more robust action is needed to enhance the spirit and to connect with God. Once the connection is made and once an approach is taken to enhance the connection—for example, using prayers from other nations, from indigenous peoples, or from a time before people took the mystical practices out of religion—worshippers today can individualize their practice of prayer. What does individualizing look like? One can light a candle, go outside, play light music, be in the bath or shower—there is no set way to pray except to sit and connect to the one above. Some will scoff at this idea of being quiet, and no one knows why, but those who also still have the spark within you will know this calling is one that you cannot refuse.

The second part of this book is about how you connect the prayer practice to your everyday life. Once you begin to pray, once you begin to individualize your actions, and once you incorporate prayer fully, you will need to make it part of you in a way that is not seen today in modern society.

What does that look like? It looks like praying as part of your life and becoming a fortress no matter what is going on. We scoff

at those who take time for prayer, such as our brothers and sisters of
Islam, who pray five times a day. This is something we should look
at more carefully. If we have prayer time in the morning, and it is
just as important as the coffee and exercise we will get up for at 4:00
a.m. so as not to miss it, prayer will find its place too. The intent here
is that when you get up, it is the norm in a household to have quiet
prayer. It is as much as a ritual as going to the bathroom first thing;
it just happens, and it is not questioned. If someone visits your home
it is one of the things you tell them will happen, just as you explain
to a guest what coffee is available and how to use the coffee maker.

This is not a far-off topic. Many, many people are practicing
meditation in this way, and there is no need to apologize for this
purposeful shift, making a direct, intentional connection with God.
Sit quietly, and let God make an intentional connection with you.
Nothing is as sweet and precious. It is a sad state of affairs that a
book like this has to be written to urge even clergy and church
people to sit quietly. We might expect our leaders in churches and
worshipping institutions to be leading this charge. Instead, we have
differences of peoples and religions in conflict, without many even
raising a voice that calls for peace.

We need this prayer to first bring a sense of God to this world
and second to bring this world to God. Loved you are and have been
since the dawn of time—and still we are convinced that we have the
power and control within our mind's eyes. Technology is abounding,
creation of food from genes or even control of human body parts,
but no one has the time to sit and let God love them.

At this time, I will address biblical scholars who have picked
apart the Bible and made a great deal of money and conversation
about what is written. Please look at the Psalms of prayer during the
time you give yourself to the one above. The Bible is a book and a
guide, and as mentioned before it has humans' hands all over it.
Spend the time you have in study to sit quietly. It is expected some
of you will attack this writing and the writer, and let it be known

now that critical action is very unhelpful in this basic text asking for prayer. May God continue to help you see the vision of his glory. These words are written specifically for those who when they read it will know the Lord is calling you back to commune. Heed this paragraph, and take the time to have God use you too to take on this charge.

This ends the prayer section of this book. The language may seem strong in places, and it is intentional writing in the way the Lord means it to be. Take stock of your prayer life. To paraphrase Jesus in the New Testament do not stand idly, speaking loudly to show off or make money, using pomp and circumstance of yourself in the name of prayer. This text has the same sentiment.

Know the reason for your prayer. The reason is to connect earnestly and humbly with God. It is quite simple. A word for those who do not believe in God: God loves and believes in you. If you should come to sit quietly to center your day without thought, the love of all love is there, no matter what you believe. Other words, it is not necessary to believe to connect. I would hope non-believers also heed the other sections of this text. All that is written here is meant as a guide of renewal and great connection to a more purposeful time in the world.

Judgment

Our next topic is judgment. A lot can be written about judgment, but especially in this day and age judgment has taken a new leaf. The definition of judgment is the taking stock of another person's actions, life, etc. and making comments, thoughts, and assumptions about the person. Basically, judgment is making any kind of assumption about a person, place, or thing and stating an opinion, which is usually negative. It would be wonderful if people were making positive statements about their neighbors, but that is not the case.

On a regular basis, negative, hurtful messages are thought, said, printed, projected on media, and even communicated in a person's face in the name of entertainment.

This rise of judgment at the entertainment level, social media level, and day-to-day level has gotten to a point of self-destruction. Why is it natural to judge your brother and sister at the drop of a hat? This behavior has to stop and be immediately curbed. To prevent judgment, we all need to love ourselves. The thing about judgment is that when you judge another, you are projecting and judging yourself. The scripture that says, "Judge ye not, old man" is not about an old man. It is saying stop hurting yourself. Stop tearing your flesh, which is the definition of sarcasm which is a form of judgment. Why would we want to tear our flesh? Let's face it. We would not, yet sarcasm is very popular. It is so popular, the very act is projected on children's programing at such a high rate that it is not monitored or curbed.

The act of judgment has sent our spiritual growth to a new low. When every form of communication is grounded in something as hurtful as sarcasm and judgment, we are missing the mark by a large margin. This is not just a fad or something that will pass; unfortunately, it has taken root in our society. What can we do about it? The solution stems from the individual level; hence this book is being sent into the world as a tool to notice and intervene.

First, stop and pay attention to the judgment in your life. I will break this up into several working categories. The first category is what you think. Are you thinking judging thoughts? You are what you think, and you think what you do. The first assessment is to go through your day and notice if you are creating judgment thought about anything. That is a wide-open field. Think about it: are you judging anything? For example, you are driving and the person in the car next to you is grooming or (pick any of the following) shaving, picking their nose, putting on makeup, or reading or texting or watching a video on the phone. What is the first thing that pops into your head? "What the heck?" Right? Then comes the heavy outpouring of judgment: "What is wrong with them?"

Stop there. That is where you need to stop the thinking train. Pause. This is going to be a difficult thing to do. Stop there. Why are you judging them? Are you afraid you are going to get hurt by their lack of attention on the road? If that is true, why not a prayer of protection for them and yourself? Why the attack? The attack has come so instantaneously that there is no pause time or even a section of grace that can enter. This has to change. First, be willing to look at this issue. Then notice how many times a day you are participating in judgment, originating judgment, or allowing judgment messages to freely come within your personal being. The answers will be alarming.

Let's look at another example of judgment at the foundational level. When we see a person, place, or thing that has taken an action that we find alarming, what do we think or do? For example, we have pageants where woman are judged by the things they say, what they wear, and how they look. We reward these women and in turn teach our most precious commodity, our children, that it is okay to judge women. Let's be frank here. The treatment of women has been and continues to be one of the sorest points in the world today, although we clearly teach this ideal to children at a very young age and fail to see where and how we are institutionalizing judgment in their daily lives.

As for judging clothing, it is more than likely right now you are thinking about women's clothing. I hope you see the connection at the foundational level. We as a society have very set ideas that have been instituted in our upbringing and life that it is okay to judge people's clothing. This is what I mean by foundational. Think about this. There is an entire institution called fashion, in which some people create clothing trends, and other people judge and manufacture these clothes for the masses. Before you can even blink, it is natural to fall into judgment as a way of life. Yet this writing is not about clothes, cars, or the actions of someone in their car at the stoplight. This writing is to help you pause, breathe, and *stop* using judgment as part of your thinking and lifestyle. The intention is to stop it. Say *no* to judgment. The hope is that you will try this experiment of monitoring yourself, and when the mental attack of another person, place, thing, or idea comes up—and it will—instead of thinking the thought all the way through, you will *stop* and say a prayer for yourself and whatever you are judging.

Sadly, when you judge, you are judging yourself. It is a projection of self-hatred. This text is about self-love. You are loved and in essence are meant to project love. There are those who will want to argue the point along this line: "How about when I pick out my car, new clothes, a college, etc., should I not make assessments?" Those points will not be addressed here because such an argument misses the point entirely. If those are the thoughts and arguments that rise to the surface after reading this, then you are not ready for this text. Go back to the section on prayer, and spend some time reading some of the indigenous sayings or poems or prayers until you are able to make that quiet connection. When you return to this section, you will understand what is being communicated here. Love yourself by not judging others in any way. Love.

Along the same line as the women's example another at the foundational level is how we view, comment on, and judge bodies in general, bodybuilders, and models. This is a common pastime. Magazines are created for men and woman to judge how one looks on the outside. This is an important note and part of our problem today. Judgment lives on the surface of our faces, our bodies, and our clothes, cars, homes, and employment. Judgment is everywhere, and one cannot escape from it. That is why it is important to note judgment from the foundational level and see it for what it is. It will be very difficult to do and if you have read this far into the text, you have a desire and will to try.

Here is your first exercise in ridding yourself of judgment.

Be kind to yourself. You probably did not expect that previous statement. Yes, be kind to yourself. To begin this practice, do not say or think anything that is detrimental to yourself. No negative self-talk, no name-calling of yourself out loud or in your head. This will be very difficult to do. Once you try it, you will see the subtle judgment seeping into your mind and life. It will be a rude awakening to notice how unkind you are being to yourself. When you treat yourself in a negative manner, there is no hope of loving thy neighbor.

Some may want to blow this exercise off as not a big deal and proclaim that they've made the choice to be the way they are. It is not true. No one chooses to be unkind to themselves, hate themselves, and treat themselves harshly. If a friend was saying what you are saying to yourself in your head, you would want to protect your friend. I am asking you to protect yourself.

Once you have gotten this far in the reading, hopefully you have participated in a prayer practice, and you have received the precious gift of serenity that would allow you to take these next steps. Do not be discouraged, it is difficult not to attack yourself; yet once your mind is quiet and peaceful, it should be easier. This is the point where it would be helpful to be in practice with a friend or partner. Community is the form of togetherness and mirroring the physical oneness we should have with God, so it is a good step. Practice with a friend by checking in with one another, praying with one another, and being in nature with one another in the name of being closer to God. Talk about judgment and how hard it is to stop by yourself.

What I am saying is that after the point of prayer and a connection, one should work on finding a community that can also support your learning and healthy practices. Notice, I did not recommend a church. This text is not anti-church—quite the opposite—but not all churches are created equal, and today the church tenets have often left behind the very people who need help.

Start sharing with a friend first. The community part starts when you are with another.

Don't overthink it. Do not start writing rules and guidelines; those are left-brain tactics and do not evoke spirit or spiritual practices. Watch for the need to overly structure or control your connection and new practice not to judge yourself. If you struggle and find yourself being unkind to yourself on a regular basis with no foundation to stop, begin to ask in your quiet time for healing in this area. You may think something like *Higher Being, God, Mother Earth or Jehovah, can you help me to love myself?* during your quiet time. Try writing a letter to your *Higher Self,* and ask for the meanness to stop; ask for love instead of meanness.

Judgment is so complex that these very simplistic steps are the first steps in getting to the core of the problem. If it were easy to stop judging people, this book would not be needed. It will take everything you have to make a conscious effort to stop judging as well as to stop condemning those who judge as a form of entertainment and or pass time. We are better than this; we are. There are many great qualities about people, and we sell ourselves short consistently by treating ourselves and our neighbors badly.

Bodies

We have become a body-focused society. Our weight, height, hair color, muscles, etc., have taken over our thoughts. When is the last time you heard someone talking about the spirit when you were not in church? The spirit has been neglected. Like a child who has been left alone, our spirits are thirsty for food, nourishment, and water. Headlines fill the airways of destruction, death, fires, and loss, but nothing—absolutely nothing—is said about the spirit.

Our spirits are our souls, and our souls need care. Our souls need nourishment. Our souls need God and a connection with God.

Prayer will lead the way, and the absence of a judgmental attitude will fertilize the soil. The next part will be the grand entrance of oneness; it will be love. Once one has made a good attempt at prayer and dismissing judgment, the role of love will be more apparent in your life, and the need to justify the world as it is will disappear.

This is the first installment of many small installments of writings which are intended for the nourishment of the soul and reconnection back to your original home with the one; you are part of the Lord. For those who are atheist or agnostic, this is to clear the channel to carry out the act of love on earth. If your intent is to be kind and loving and to assist others when you can, then you too can follow the simple path of taking quiet time, communing with nature, stopping judgment, and loving more abundantly. Although God, Jesus, Mother Earth and other descriptions are mentioned in this discussion, realize that everyone can connect with the actions that are suggested here. It is by no means exclusive to *anyone*. This message is for everyone. I hope that is clear. In the section of poems, literature, and global prayers there is something for every soul who is seeking.

Communities of Support

If you have enjoyed this work and find that it has spoken to you and helped you in some way, please share it with a friend. This is the part of the text that leads to communities with other people. It is best to be with people who understand and can basically support each other. This is not a study group. That is not the intention of this text. It is simply a guide to prayer, lack of judgment, and more community.

As mentioned earlier, the church has not been the refuge for people to enter. As people age, the number of people who do attend are attending for the wrong reasons. Many believe a connection with God is something that people has put in front of them and do not feel the loving peace of God in their lives. This is not an absolute. There are those who are connected to God, and it is easy to notice who they are in society. Really be earnest with yourself: are you connected to a community that supports quiet time with God, lack of judgment at a gut level, and a love that superimposes itself over hate and fear? If you are in that kind of community, great! Please recruit more people, and use this book as a guide. In actuality such communities are few and far between, and not many have access to them. I am not referring to yoga, exercise, or reading groups. This is for prayer, lack of judgment, love, and gathering.

When you are ready to begin your group, start with one or two people. It does not have to be large. Begin your meeting with connection to each other, sitting quietly; dim the lights, and set a timer. Set a timer as a way to manage your time and set the space for prayer. I am not suggesting any pomp and circumstance, incense, candles, etc. There is a place for such things, but the world has gone way overboard with that process. Sit and pray. That's it.

Later, break bread and talk about the struggles of not judging and how you have loved people more. It is pretty simple, and I am not suggesting a big to-do. I am suggesting the opposite—a pot of soup and bread, a small discussion, and the evening is over. This may be the oddest request you have ever gotten, but that is it. Make sure that the place where you are is quiet; no televisions, radios, or babbling brooks—just quiet. That is the first step in creating community. Only those who have connected and understand will be willing to come and gather. My prayer is that many will start these loving circles of truth to dismantle preconceived thinking about truth, prayer, and love. This is the first of many installments, they are small for a reason to easily digest and enact. Blessings to you, and continued journey to spiritual health, love, and connection to the one cares for us all. Peace.

The previous illustrations were made as a way to get started. This section will be a continuation of the thoughts of the previous text. As you may recall, the last text was about beginning to rekindle a relationship with a higher self or God. This text will be about how to deepen those practices. It may not seem like more information is needed, but it is. Leveling one's pride and humbling oneself to daily practice is not easy yet, and the consistency of leaning into this way of living will be difficult.

The day-to-day happenings in the world today can be hard to avoid, and the very things that are being addressed are the perpetrators of more confusion. This section will address social media, television and movies, and children's books and movies. This may seem like the same category, entertainment, but what you think is connected to what you do, and what today's people think is associated with entertainment and media. It is very difficult to pray, love, and create community when today's entertainment is telling you otherwise. I think that the lack of prudence, attention, or care to what goes into our bodies and psyches is most troubling and concerning. When was the last time you turned away or paused and said, "This is not for me," or "I do not like the theme of what is going on"? How about "This is so dark; I do not want to subject my senses to it"? I would guess not lately. At this time, we seem to digest sick images, words, and themes consistently and question nothing.

The saddest thing is that we also project these same images onto our innocent children. Children are pure and void of the world when they are taken to movies as infants. It is time to think about what we are doing to our children. What images we are putting into their minds at young ages. Children are attending movies as early as one, two, and three. Most times the parent or caretaker has not seen the movie or read about its theme. Today many films and TV shows have adult themes and messages in them. What a shame that we allow such images to pass through the lives of our children. I feel very strongly about this and always have. My children did not watch

TV. I picked their show (one show) and recorded it for the weekend. If or when the children had time they could watch some of the show, and I sat down with them to watch it. As a single parent at the time, I did not want the ideals, thoughts, and morals of the television shows to guide the thinking of my young children. The commercials alone could cause harm to their young psyches.

Social media amount to a phenomenon that has a life of its own. Attached to money, property, and prestige on one end and inward-facing self-centeredness on the other, the whole ball of wax is quite troubling. In moderation there are things that really stand out to send images and thoughts of peace, love, and joy. Then there are the dark parts of communication and sharing that we all can cringe from examining. I hope I can make clear without the silent time of prayer something as simple as a picture of a child in need becomes something else entirely. All sickness known to man is expanded with social media, and we have become a world that has no center rooted in a spirit connection. Something as simple as a picture can simply take on a dark presence because souls are thirsty for something, and darkness is easy to grab. Most people do not know they are thirsty.

The increase of social media accounts has overtaken communication in a way and this is really unhealthy. Children as young as ten or even younger are entertained by such media platforms and encouraged to do things that yield them financial gain. Are we paying attention to this? How can you easily look away? When Jesus entered the temple and people were having a swap meet, he went crazy on them for not respecting and holding reverence in the space. Today, we are constantly having a swap meet in our minds with social media and have not noticed it at all.

We walk through judgment and participate in polls on matters that are not our business. We give our opinion where it does not matter, nor is it useful to our continued spiritual growth. Never do we pause and think about the things we need to do for our own health and spiritual well-being. That is why these writings are so important because we have let ourselves go. No, we have given ourselves away. Yes, we have been giving ourselves away and did not even have a chance. It is heartbreaking. With judgment as the backbone, social media is the vehicle to judge second by second without leaving your home, table, bed, or car.

The rack is so large that a persona can be developed that is a creation outside of your true self, and that character will provide you with fame, fortune, and attention. For example, take the iconic Angelyne. This Los Angeles icon was displayed on billboards in Los Angeles as a pin up girl beginning in 1984. The blond and buxom woman barely clad was stretched across huge billboards on major intersections. You saw her whether you wanted to or not.

This is what is happening in social media. I remember looking at the billboards and wondering, *Who is this, and why do I have to see this?* Social media today is the same. You may have some power over what you see, but mostly you do not. That being said, it is imperative in this day and age that we protect what is good and peaceful in all of us. That is the purpose of this portion of the writing. What is peaceful in you, and have you talked to that part of yourself lately?

What do you do? First, you establish quiet time daily as described in the first section of this writing. Second, you intentionally stop judging people, places, and things. Lastly, you cultivate relationships with others who are on the same path as you. When you are able to establish this foundation, pulling back from social media will not seem like a difficult task. On social media, look for and be drawn to things that are not sad news stories about other people's challenges, sensationalism, gossip, or images that represent those things. Yes, this will be a barrier at first, but it is easily overcome, as you will be repelled from such content. Friends or followers who frequently post such content should be removed, blocked, or hidden. The feed of your viewing will look different.

After you have completed that task, reduce your time on social media altogether. Ask yourself as you are engaging, *Is this nice? Do*

I want this image, story, or post in my body? Most times the answer will be no, and you will learn to step away and not put your spirit through such turmoil.

What do you put in its place? More time in nature. To spend more time being immersed in and enhanced by nature will rock your world. Don't scoff. Nature is a connection to the universe in a way that nothing else is, and we who are slowing down and just being will benefit from the amazing pleasure of being in nature. Try it. Take a walk in nature; sit and watch nature, and I am not referring to nature shows. I am referring to actual nature. More on that subject in the next installment.

Movies and television are a problem in modern society. The images, thoughts, and ideas are disturbing, and the rate at which these ideas enter the body and mind is astounding. The kinds of movie entertainment and television that enter your body have to be monitored. Much like social media, the gruesome images, blood, destruction, body violations, and implications of fear are off the charts. We call it entertainment, and we are not tethered to a higher self, higher power, or God. This kind of imagery is nothing but destructive to our souls.

Take an inventory of what you are doing in this area. For two weeks write down the movies and television you watch. What you will see is the influx of violence, sadness, and fear-based situations presented as entertainment and fun. You will not see light, joy, peace, wisdom, or unconditional love. Think of that for a moment. Is this what you want in your body, mind, or psyche? You become what you consume, and at this rate many of us are not going to connect to the good, positive parts of ourselves at all in this lifetime.

There are whole genres of movies devoted to violence. The *Kill Bill* series is an example. When did entertainment become how many people can be killed in the most gruesome of ways? If you are thinking, *I don't watch that kind of film*, what about horror, depressing dramas, war, or movies where a string of bad things continues to happen? Take a really honest look. I know these themes are prevalent because we reward them yearly. Every year the Oscars have less and less joy and more and more depictions of worldly strife. Why?

What can you do instead of watching endless hours of television? Spend time in nature, reading inspirational materials, being of service to those in need, or basically loving one another. This is the basis of our work here: to love. We have lost our way, so much so that loving one another is not an option or a thought. What is an option or a thought is whether we are going to have the money we need, whether our child is going to be most prepared for the best college, and our individualistic wants, desires, and perceived needs. This is nothing like loving one another.

Television and movies have taken each individual to the most extreme state of godless consciousness. Coupled with the actions of the church through the years, the academia of the Bible, and the rejection of mystical practices and beliefs, people today are very much counting on their worldly selves as the alpha and omega. We are very much off the beam. This writing is the strongest of suggestions. Television that is not inspirational and brings no joy and happiness must be stopped—not reduced, but stopped.

It is very simple. Is the message one of joy, happiness and connection to the universe? If not, do not put it into your body. Much like a bad drug or poison, we are at the point of emergency. Try it. Do not engage in any negative social media and television while praying, reading special inspiring indigenous texts, and engaging with nature. The point is that if you are different, if your thoughts are different, your connection of oneness to your higher self will be different. To be very clear, this is regarding all entertainment that is negative, dark, and debilitating.

Lastly, this next section is about what we allow our children to see and digest in the world. Our children are our most precious commodity.

Enlightened to join the earthly world, we should protect them from negative images and learning while they are being indoctrinated into this world. What that means is that everything they hear, see, smell, and understand becomes part of their foundational being.

There are infants who are taken to theaters and exposed to loud action movies. This has a destructive effect on the nervous system and processing parts of the body. The view seems widespread that children just born are ready for outside simulation right away. Think about days gone by, when children did not have access to the lighting, media, and sounds we have today. Protect your children from overstimulation of the senses. They may become accustomed to the input, and it tunes their foundational senses to a high vibration that is not conducive to peace and connection to their higher self.

Parents use television, tablets, and media as babysitters for children as a form of taking a break or getting some time to themselves. We should rethink what we put in front of our children. Messages of loving one another, kindness, and nature's wonders are better than fast-moving shows with flashing lights and loud sounds. Also consider the commercials that are shown during a television show. Beyond their high stimulating effects, these can be inappropriate because the implications of gender, morals, and worldliness are at a high.

Be discerning ahead of time about any movie you take your child to see. Discern the age of your child and their developmental maturity before you put them in front of a large screen of input. Watch, read up, or study the media you are proposing for your child. Many sources of information explain in detail what the film is about, the areas of concern for children, and recommendations.

One thing that I am really pounding home here is that there is nothing protecting children. These things happen because of parents' wants and needs. This is inappropriate for our children. Protect them, nurture them, love them, and teach them love and how to love. Use these phrases as a guide to monitor and protect them when it comes to media, television, and any input of senses into their bodies. Children require the ability to be free, love, and play. Look at the things they are doing and ask yourself if you are allowing them to be free souls. If you have every minute of their day tied up with activities, it is not good for them or yourself. Moderation is key here.

Use the same moderation with yourself and your precious soul. As mentioned before, social media, television, and even radio can be spirit depleters. If you are depleting your spirit, what are you doing to uphold it? Nourishment should include being in nature, praying, and serving others. These are not the only things one can do, but they are the focus of this text. What have you done, or how often do you follow these nourishing pursuits? This is your check point. If the answer is no, then there is work to be done.

This text will only speak to those who are ready and willing to walk toward more enlightenment. They will take these words and continue to seek the connection of oneness with God. Take the action, and the rest will follow.

This is the end of a short combination of guides and stories to assist in one thing only: oneness connection to God, Allah, Jehovah, Mother Nature, the Divine, the Universe, etc. Use it to do so. If you have questions reach out, and they will be answered. May the peace of the Lord, the Universe, or the Great Spirit and the healing forces that pull us into oneness keep you and connect you to the source that is all powerful, you.

Chapter 3

Welcome back to the series on the connection with God or your higher self. Hopefully you have read the previous text to prepare yourself for this section. Here you will explore a bit farther along your journey of self-realization and walk toward a more peaceful and serene lifestyle. As in the previous text, the first step toward more connection with the God that dwells inside of you is to pray.

Prayer was described as sitting quiet to allow your true consciousness to connect. This is something that requires a consistent commitment and dedication. The previous text laid out suggestions on how to begin. If you have now begun your journey, a group of like-minded friends are in place, and prayer is carried on at the group level as well.

The communion of friends is the community of love and togetherness for the continued nourishment of your soul. The church was intended to be the place for this togetherness. The church refers to the places where people gather, not necessarily the Christian faith in particular. It may be the mosque, temple, home, or any place where people gather with the goal of connecting to a higher self.

Try to avoid thinking in dualistic thoughts, this-or-that thinking. Such thinking very much pulls away from the spiritual connections of your higher self. In this stage, you will move into service to the world, grow your conscious contact in such a way that it is readily available like a soothing blanket, and learn to mentor others who are on this journey of self-discovery.

To review what has been previously written, prayer is the mainstay of connection to God or your highest self, which is God. The name you use is not important; Mother Nature, the higher self, Allah, Jehovah, the Great Spirit, and the Divine are just a few examples of names. Do not get lost in the weeds the actual connection is the important part here. In the previous text, we discussed how to connect and what tenets to use to stay connected.

Judgment is a tendency that has to be interrupted. If you are this far into these readings, you know that judgement of yourself, anyone, or anything is corrosive and not aligned with spiritual practice. I write this here because some may skip the other reading and try to start here. Judgment of any kind works against the connection with your higher self. Go back to earlier sections to read and study more on how to begin not to allow this corrosive thread to rule your life. Media, movies, and television are instruments of the world today that help to perpetuate judgment, self-hatred, and continued disconnection.

It also is important to note here that influences on children were mentioned in previous writings. Our most precious and innocent souls, children, are ingesting media, television, and movies at an alarming rate. This constant stream of values are not aligned with the connectedness to a higher power; it is the opposition. On the other hand, we have children who are subjected to hate rhetoric, taught to use the Bible in a divisive way, and live lives that separate them from the source of God as love.

Using the earlier writings as foundational learning; this next phase is to build on what you started there. Welcome again to the communion of oneness in the form of connection to your higher self; this journey is an exciting one. By now you have felt the spirit within and have bathed in the peace and comfort of sitting in those quiet moments. If you have not felt the warmness I am describing, let's get you there. First, how do you deepen the prayer and connection you have started? Your practice at this point should include daily prayer time. You may possibly use a reading to ground yourself, a scripture, or anything that calls to you as inspirational. A candle or incense may be lit and quiet music may play as you sit clearing your mind.

The mind is the thing that must be mastered. Your mind will try to take you into places that are seemingly important at the time—a grocery list, what someone said at work, or that thing you always need to do. Discipline your mind to follow your wishes. This is not an easy feat; many of our great spiritual leaders of today spend much time in prayer and quiet time. This is necessary to master the mind to move into spiritual thought instead of worldly thought.

When will you know if you are getting there? Once you sit quiet, an amazing thing happens: nothing. You are at peace, and the time has flown by. This is an indicator you are on the right track. In the beginning you will use a timer, and if you are progressing a timer will seem like a hindrance. The time you spend will seem refreshing and invigorating. You will want it more and more.

Once you have created a community for connection, you will begin to fellowship, pray, and discuss the connection process and rewards. Many people today are doing so. Brother Richard Rohr is one who has created a community of connection to the higher self, and once you begin to walk on this journey, others will naturally show up who are on the same path. Once you get there, it is time to enhance and maintain your practices.

The first part of maintaining your practice is to expand your knowledge about spiritual matters and the connection you seek. Here the hoop is very wide; be curious about such matters, and seek those that call to you. There is not a prescription for how you should go deeper. Each should have their own journey. What I am saying here is that if you are at this point in your practice, you are praying regularly, not judging yourself or others, moderating social media and entertainment, and communing with a group of people and discussing your practice. The next step is to study spiritual information that calls to you. Each person is different, and there is no set study. How exciting! When you get to this point of your enhancement, various communities will make themselves known to you because you will be drawn to them.

Your service to others is very important. This is not the kind of service that one would do and walk away, such as giving money to the homeless. This service to others is based on your ability to deeply love yourself and not focus habitually on worldly matters. The deepest service you can give is the connection to your highest self and the ability to love one another. This thought seems very familiar because it has been mentioned several times and many ways in Jesus's teaching and parables, yet it is the continued struggle of this century more than ever.

Love is a universal spiritual tool that is the foundation of the connection with God. Humans on this plane have seen, used, and abused it for something it is not. "Love one another" begins with loving yourself—not in a selfish and self-centered way but because in your times of prayer, you are making the deepest connections to your higher self, and you are projecting that love to everyone, no matter how they act or what they say. Yes, this is quite an order. Treat yourself lovingly by getting into the space of quiet time so deeply that you are feeling that warm glow. It is so needed and wanted.

Love is an industry in today's world. Driven by profit margins and reality TV shows, love is something to sell, to abuse. The twisted thought of love as sexual is very perverse and saddening to the world. Simplify yourself rooted in your daily practice, and deeply love yourself. This means that any thoughts that dominate you and tell you repeatedly that you are worthless are not part of this process. All negativity in thought, word, and deed must stop, and they will diminish when you stop judging people and yourself.

If this was an easy task, it would have happened by now, and this text would not be necessary. How do you love yourself? Begin with the earlier text, and practice until you feel you are ready to move on. Every day, give your thinking to the Great Spirit, higher self, or Holy Spirit. In a prayer you can write or say you want every thought, idea, and action to be decided by spirit, and if there is not time for you to ask for help, that help will be given to you.

Here is a prayer written by Gary Renard in *3 Easy Ways to Undo Your Ego, Heal Your Life*: "Holy Spirit, you be in charge. You direct my thoughts all day. If there's no time for me to ask you what to think then I know you have promised that wisdom will be given me when I need it. What I do is just a result of what I think, and I trust you to guide me." This is a good prayer for you to use or write to fit your needs. It grounds you in connectedness daily.

Start by not participating in any negative thoughts about others or yourself. This will be a challenge because the part of you that does not love you will try to convince you that there are problems that need to be addressed. This is our biggest struggle: maintaining control of our minds. That is why it is important to establish prayer and connection as your base. Coming from the place of connection will change everything. Interactions, conversations, and struggle will look and feel different when you are not fretting or frantic. Peace beyond all understanding grounded in the grace of goodness will be your new experience.

Take another round of excluding the nuances that bring judgment and apartness in your life. Start by examining how you spend your day. How much is on your device? How many negative articles or posts are you digesting? How many pictures of heartbreaking scenes are you observing as you scroll aimlessly through your phone? What kind of judgments are you reading, seeing, or discussing about what other people are doing or not doing? How much emotion is in your voice when you point these things out to others? These questions are guidelines toward inner peace.

After you have made yourself a clear vessel of goodness, you are ready to serve the world in another way. It is important to note drugs and alcohol here. Many push their reality by drinking excessively or using drugs in what can be called a recreational way. To be able to connect clearly, your system cannot be influenced with drugs and alcohol. I want to be very clear here. There are souls who claim the glory of God who are under the influence while doing so. This is not what I am describing. I am describing true connection with God, your higher self, in such a way that you are daily guided in good and service to yourself and others. Beware of those who claim to connect with quick schemes, the magic cure, or answers that come from above. These are frauds who capitalize on the idea that people do not know themselves (their Self) and will be easily manipulated.

Once you have ensured the strength of your connection and removed another layer of judgmental practices, it is time to purge those glaring and nagging hindrances of past harms done to you. The areas where one must forgive. Even if you think you have moved on, it is important to forgive everyone and everything. No matter how small it may seem to you, you have to love and forgive.

This world holds many ideas of "not fair." These ideas are roadblocks to freedom. It seems the ideas of safety and forgiveness are at odds, and it simply is not so. The depth of forgiveness lives in your subconscious and in your soul. If you feel again the same way you did when the harm occurred, you have not forgiven. Take time to examine each area of forgiveness or offense from various perspectives. Let out all of your feelings about the situation. Then let it go. This is a very simplistic way to express it; you have to forgive in the depths of your soul, and let it go with love. I will spend more time on this topic in a future writing. If you are stuck on this topic, the great writings and work by Gary Renard would be helpful. Do not push these feelings away and think you will be able to be of service. This area of forgiveness is vital for connectedness and oneness.

Once you feel you have established a consistent connection

and moved from the glaring harms of others into forgiveness, it is time to serve the world and your community at large. What exactly does that mean? More than ever, it means to continue to grow your learning through fellowship with others who are seeking oneness. Multitudes of people are lost and not connected, trying as they might to find whatever way they can to serve. It is much like people walking in circles. Enhance your groups with prayer, forgiveness, nonjudgmental practices, and nature enhancement. Include children to be involved in your prayer time and ways of being. Be of service by becoming the shining light of oneness in your daily walk of life.

This practical way of being will become natural and life will change. The lack of input from negativity and judgment will ease the burden of worldly things and life. The ability to experience peace and love daily as well as have the essence of peace and love within your circles of friends will feel freeing. The ability to love yourself truly will come into view.

The next step on this journey is to deepen your prayer practice and the self-care and love of yourself. This may seem selfish or unrealistic, but it is not. The deep love of yourself reflects the deep love of the God within you. I anticipate if you have read to this point that you have some kind of self-love or self-care practice, and I know how strong the thoughts of self-loathing and judgment can be. This corrosive seed must be removed in us, body, mind, and spirit. The thoughts that arise in our brain about ourselves and other people, the thoughts about ourselves and the stream of negativity, have to be replaced by love. It is quite that simple. Love is and has been the foundation of our being. Although these words are not many, they are powerful and will require all you have to complete and adhere to them.

Start at the beginning of the text, and review often how your prayer life is working for you. Examine your judgment toward yourself and others. Pay attention to the media, social media, and entertainment you put into your body and spirit. Pay special attention to all children and young souls; they too need a connection to God, and although they are each very close, the constant media and entertainment messages pull them away. Lose yourself in nature, relish it, and breathe it in. Establish groups and communities of those living the same way. Participate in groups of prayer and learning. Help one another live this way, and love all, even those who bring harms. You will become the oneness that you seek. Stop looking for the thing that fixes you. You are it. Find yourself.

Structure your life much as you would if you did not want to get sick. When you are being careful to avoid illness, you sleep more, drink lots of fluids, and cut out any extra activity. This is the same as when you are aligning with God within yourself. Keep spiritual literature easily at hand, and remove yourself from harmful media, socializing, and people. Protect the precious jewel that you are, the same way you would protect a child. If you have made it this far into the work, you have done well and now feel wholeness, peace, and oneness at a new level. Avail yourself of works that will enhance your state of oneness with God.

References

Anderson, B., and D. Howe. (2019) In *The Woman's Book of Prayer: 365 Blessings, Poems and Meditations*. Mango Media. (Essay on pp. 117–117.)

Angels. Lord of Angels. (n.d.) Retrieved August 14, 2021, from https://lordofangels.weebly.com/angels.html.

Chief Yellow Lark (Trans.). (n.d.) The Great Spirit Prayer - Akta Lakota Museum & Cultural Center. Retrieved July 4, 2021, from http://aktalakota.stjo.org/site/News2?page=NewsArticle&id=8580.

Church Hymnal Corp. (1979) *The Book of Common Prayer and administration of the sacraments and other rites and ceremonies of the Church: together with the Psalter of Psalms of David according to the use of the Episcopal Church: proposed.* (Prayer 58.)

Dimtsu, G. (2008) Do not forsake us Etegdefene.

Egudu, & Nwoga Heinemann Educational Books. (n.d.) *Home*. African Poems. Retrieved July 6, 2021, from https://africanpoems.net/gods-ancestors/morning-prayer-igbo/.

Forward Day By Day. (n.d.) *Prayers and Thanksgivings*. Daily Prayer: a resource of Forward Movement: Morning Resolve. Retrieved

July 4, 2021, from https://prayer.forwardmovement.org/prayers_ and_thanksgivings.php.

Foster, R. J., and B. Smith. (2005) *Devotional Classics: Selected Readings for Individuals and Groups*. Renovare. Retrieved July 4, 2021, from https://renovare.org/books/devotional-classics.

Fulay. (n.d.). *Ancient Egyptian prayers and ritual worship - Tutankhamun project - 6th period (fulay)*. Google Sites-Ancient Egyptian prayers and ritual worship - Tutankhamun project. Retrieved August 14, 2021, from https://sites.google.com/a/ smpanthers.org/fulay-6th-period-scripture/home/ancient-egyptian-prayers-and-ritual-worship.

Hoban, K. (2010, December) *Affirmations: "I am fearless."* Prayers, Mantras & Spiritual Lyrics. Retrieved August 15, 2021, from https://prayersmantrasspirituallyrics.wordpress.com/?s= affirmations.

Holy Bible: New Revised Standard Version: containing the Old and New Testaments and the Deuterocanonical Books. (2005) Hendrickson Bibles.

Kavasch, E. B. (2002) In *The medicine wheel garden: creating sacred space for healing, celebration, and tranquility*. Bantam Books. (Kindle Locations 4823–4830.)

Kett, G. (n.d.) *Page: A Treasury of South African poetry.djvu/294*. Wikisource, the free online library. Retrieved August 14, 2021, from https://en.wikisource.org/wiki/Page:A_Treasury_of_South_ African_Poetry.djvu/294.

Killoran, R. M. (2008) Every time I turn around, I hear more words of war … Retrieved July 4, 2021, from https://www.

worldprayers.org/archive/prayers/invocations/every_time_i_turn_around.html.

Law, W. (2010) *Courage to Change*. Al-Anon Family Groups (Aust).

Lim, E. (2010, December) *Affirmations:* Prayers, Mantras & Spiritual Lyrics. Retrieved August 15, 2021, from https://prayersmantrasspirituallyrics.wordpress.com/?s=affirmations.

Madaras, B. (n.d.) Heavenly Father, I call on you … Retrieved July 4, 2021, from https://www.worldprayers.org/archive/prayers/invocations/heavenly_father_i_call_on.html.

Mansfield, K. (2010) In *Courage to change*. Al-Anon Family Groups (Aust). (Essay, p. 255,)

Mishkan T'filah. (n.d.) *Shehecheyanu*. New York: CCAR Press. Reform Judaism. Retrieved July 4, 2021, from https://reformjudaism.org/beliefs-practices/prayers-blessings/shehecheyanu.

Mychal Judge's Prayer. Irish Franciscans. (2013, September 11) Retrieved July 4, 2021, from https://www.franciscans.ie/mychal-judge-s-prayer/.

Narasimhaye. (2014, March 22) *Prayer*. Narasimhaye's Blog. Retrieved August 15, 2021, from https://narasimhaye.wordpress.com/2014/03/22/prayer/.

One Light Many Windows Collections of Wisdom. (2010, December) *Affirmations for Peace and Harmony*. Prayers, Mantras & Spiritual Lyrics. Retrieved August 15, 2021, from https://prayersmantrasspirituallyrics.wordpress.com/?s=affirmations.

One Light Many Windows Collections of Wisdom. (2014, August 17) *Daily prayers : Hinduism*. Prayers, Mantras & Spiritual Lyrics. Retrieved August 15, 2021, from https:// prayersmantrasspirituallyrics.wordpress.com/2014/08/17/ daily-prayers-of-hindus/.

Pringle, T. (n.d.) *Page: A Treasury of South African Poetry.djvu/290*. Wikisource, the free online library. Retrieved August 14, 2021, from https://en.wikisource.org/wiki/Page:A_Treasury_of_ South_African_Poetry.djvu/290.

Renard, G. (n.d.) *3 easy ways to undo your ego*. HealYourLife. Retrieved September 28, 2021, from https://www.healyourlife. com/3-easy-ways-to-undo-your-ego.

Roberts, E., & Amidon, E. (2011) Creed. In *Earth prayers: 365 prayers, poems, and invocations from around the world*. HarperOne.

Sinha, S. (2010, December) *Affirmations: Divine Expression* . Prayers, Mantras & Spiritual Lyrics. Retrieved August 15, 2021, from https:// prayersmantrasspirituallyrics.wordpress.com/?s=affirmations.

Thich Nhat Hanh. (2011, February 21) Prayers, Mantras & Spiritual Lyrics. Retrieved August 15, 2021, from https:// prayersmantrasspirituallyrics.wordpress.com/2011/02/20/ thich-nhat-hanh/.

This Week at CCLA - September 19, 2019. (n.d.) Retrieved August 14, 2021, from https://us15.campaign-archive.com/?u=9875a6772c bddbfe568bbdd26&id=940a068dca.

A Treasury of South African poetry and Verse/Religious and Metaphysical Poems. (n.d.) Wikisource, the free online library. Retrieved August 14, 2021, from https://en.wikisource.org/wiki/A_

Treasury_of_South_African_Poetry_and_Verse/Religious_
and_Metaphysical_poems.

TsleilWaututh, C. D. G. (n.d.) *A quote by Dan George*. Goodreads.
Retrieved August 14, 2021, from https://www.goodreads.com/
quotes/1238352-the-beauty-of-the-trees-the-softness-of-the-air.

Tutu, D. (1995). An African Prayer Book, A Fisherman's Song of
Praise. In *An African prayer book* (pp. Kindle Location-407–409).
essay, Doubleday.

——— (1995). An African prayer book, An African Canticle. In
An African prayer book (pp. Kindle Locations-243–251). essay,
Doubleday.

——— (1995). An African prayer book, Choirs of Praise. In *An
African prayer book* (pp. Kindle Location -376–380). essay,
Doubleday.

——— (1995). An African Prayer Book, Great Spirit. In *An African
prayer book* (pp. Kindle Locations-286–289). essay, Doubleday.

——— (1995). An African prayer book, Today is God. In *An African
prayer book* (pp. Kindle Location-252–256). essay, Doubleday.

——— (2004). A Blessing. In *An African prayer book* (Ser. Kindle
Locations 1376-1377). essay, Double Storey.

——— (2004). A Fisherman's Song of Praise. In *An African prayer
book* (Ser. Kindle Locations 407-409). essay, Doubleday.

——— (2004). An African Prayer Book, I Have No Words To Thank
You. In *An African prayer book* (pp. Kindle Locations-308–314).
essay, Doubleday.

———— (2004). An African prayer book, Love Ever Burning. In *An African prayer book* (pp. Kindle Location-276–279). essay, Doubleday.

———— (2004). Deliver Us From Fear of The Unknown. In *An African prayer book* (Ser. Kindle Locations 1170-1172). essay, Doubleday.

———— (2004). Deliver Us From Fear. In *An African prayer book* (Ser. Kindle Locations 407-409). essay, Doubleday.

———— (2004). God Free You. In *An African prayer book* (Ser. Kindle Locations 1370-1372). essay, Doubleday.

———— (2004). Make Us Instruments of Your Faith . In *An African prayer book* (Ser. Kindle Locations 1044-1046). essay, Doubleday.

———— (2004). May God Agree With Us. In *An African prayer book* (Ser. Kindle Locations 1036-1038). essay, Doubleday.

———— (2004). One Family. In *An African prayer book* (Ser. Kindle Locations 869-870). essay, Doubleday.

———— (2004). Thank You Very Much! In *An African prayer book* (Ser. Kindle Locations 784-788). essay, Doubleday.

———— (2004). The Source of Being is Above. In *An African prayer book* (pp. Kindle Locations 407–409). essay, Doubleday.

———— (2004). Victory Is Ours. In *An African prayer book* (Ser. Kindle Locations 929-930). essay, Doubleday.

———— (2004). You Have Helped My Life to Grow Like a Tree. In *An African prayer book* (Ser. Kindle Locations 618-624). essay, Doubleday.

———— (2004). You Have Prepared in Peace The Path. In *An African prayer book* (Ser. Kindle Locations 1284-1286). essay, Double Storey.

unknown. (n.d.). Daily Prayer of the Soul-nur nurbha.

Young, S. (2019). In *Jesus calling: enjoying peace in His presence.* Thomas Nelson. (Essay, pp. 549–550.)

Young, S. (2019). In *Jesus calling: enjoying peace in His presence.* Thomas Nelson. (Essay, June 22, pp. 384–385.)

Printed in the United States
by Baker & Taylor Publisher Services